Ideas of the Modern World

Anti-Capitalism

R. G. Grant

WAYLAND

Copyright © Wayland 2003

Published in Great Britain in 2003 by Hodder Wayland, a division of Hodder Children's Books.

This paperback edition published in 2007 by Wayland, an imprint of hachette Children's Books.

This book was prepared for Hodder Wayland by Patience Coster at Book Factory.

Series design: Simon Borrough
Proof reader: David C. Sills, Proof Positive Reading Services

The right of R. G. Grant to be identified as the author of this work has been asserted by him in accordance with the Copyright, Designs and Patents Act 1988.

British Library Cataloguing in Publication Data
Grant, R. G.
Anti-capitalism. - (Ideas of the modern world)
Juvenile literature
I. Title
330.1'22

ISBN 978 0 7502 4390 2

Printed in China

Hachette Children's Books
338 Euston Road, London NW1 3BH

Acknowledgements
The author and publishers thank the following for permission to reproduce photographs:

AKG London: pages 8, 9, 18, 32, 33, 45; AKG Photo: page 20; Corbis: page 29 (right); Ecoscene/Corbis: page 34 (Wayne Lawler); Wayland Picture Library/Cubafotos/John Griffiths: page 37; Wayland Picture Library/Gordon Clements: page 31; Wayland Picture Library/UPI: page 27; Mary Evans Picture Library: pages 13, 16, 21, 22, 23; Mary Evans/Tom Morgan: page 10; Popperfoto: pages 25, 28, 29 (left), 36, 43, 59; Popperfoto/Reuters: pages 4, 7, 35, 51, 52 and contents page, 55 and title page, 56, 57; Rex Features: 6, 15, 39, 41, 42, 47, 48.

Cover photo shows protesters blocking a police line from moving forward during the World Trade Organization summit in Seattle, USA on 30 November 1999 (Popperfoto).

A80320

Contents

Protest on the Streets

In November and December 1999 more than 50,000 protesters gathered on the streets of Seattle, in the north west of the United States. A summit meeting of the World Trade Organization (WTO) was being held there, attended by representatives of 135 countries, including the US president at the time, Bill Clinton. The WTO summit was intended to carry forward the process known as '**globalization**' – the means by which different economies around the world become increasingly integrated into one large economy. With globalization, trade and money flow freely from country to country. Businesses have access to a 'global market' – selling and producing their product wherever they can or wherever labour is cheapest. The global market means that businesses can have access to cheaper imports and larger export markets. But these benefits are not necessarily shared by all and, although the protesters at the WTO summit were drawn from many different groups of people, they all agreed that unrestricted global **capitalism** was to be resisted.

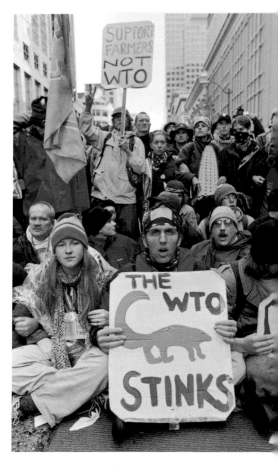

Anti-capitalist demonstrators block a street during the WTO summit in Seattle on 30 November 1999. The protests severely disrupted the summit meeting.

Making the rich richer

These anti-globalization protesters believed that globalization was being promoted by the governments of richer countries to allow big business to exploit the Earth's people and natural resources. They believed this was a policy that was making the rich richer and the poor poorer. At the same time it was destroying the environment and undermining established cultures and ways of life. The protesters felt they were standing up for ordinary people who were powerless in the face of decisions taken by the world's political and business leaders – decisions which could have a devastating effect on individual lives.

Direct attacks

A small minority of the demonstrators in Seattle were bent on carrying out direct attacks on the objects of their anger. They smashed the windows of branches of **multinational businesses** such as Starbucks, McDonalds and Gap. As the police confronted the protesters, firing plastic bullets and tear-gas, the centre of Seattle was reduced to a battleground. For a time the WTO summit was paralyzed, with senior politicians and their officials trapped in their hotels. Whereas non-violent protest might have been ignored, the violent chaos captured headlines across the world.

Seattle in 1999 was only one example of the anti-globalization demonstrations that now accompany most summit meetings of world leaders or finance ministers. Now, wherever such meetings take place, city centres are defended by heavily armed police. In the summer of 2001, during a meeting of world leaders in Genoa, Italy, a demonstrator was killed during violent clashes between protesters and police. Although only tiny numbers took part in the violence that attracted so much publicity, there was no doubt that millions of people worldwide sympathized with the protesters' hostility to the way the world was being run.

Rich against poor

One radical group, the League of Revolutionaries for a New America, declared after the 1999 protests in Seattle:

'The huge protests against the World Trade Organization's meeting in Seattle were a reflection of a confrontation which is gathering momentum – the confrontation between the world's rich and the world's poor.'

Riot police fire tear-gas to disperse demonstrators during the meeting of world leaders in Genoa, Italy, July 2001.

What is anti-capitalism?

These protest movements have often been referred to as 'anti-capitalist' (opposing capitalism). Capitalism is the **economic system** which dominates the world we live in. It is based on the idea that it is good for humankind as a whole if individuals and businesses try to make as much money as possible by selling goods and services. To do this they constantly search out new ways of producing things more cheaply, or making new products, or using new technology to produce things more efficiently.

Important to capitalism working effectively is the idea of a free market. This means having no controls or restrictions on buying and selling goods – which should mean that competition between different producers ensures that prices are

Mixed and merry

Anti-capitalism protesters glory in the diversity of the groups involved in their actions and the carnival atmosphere they generate. Richard Swift, co-editor of the radical magazine *New Internationalist*, described an anti-capitalist protest in Quebec, Canada in 2001:

'Imagination was not in short supply. A contingent [group] dressed in black-and-white uniforms marched as "Mad Cows Against Globalization". A huge Ronald McDonald swayed over the crowd with large bags of money in either hand.... There were Haitian contingents, local Mobilization for Global Justice coalitions (MOBforGLOB) from New Jersey to Ottawa, people from all over Latin America, the World March of Women, and LOLA (Little Old Lady Activists).'

Capitalism good for the poor

Writing in the solidly pro-capitalist newspaper *The Times* in March 2002, journalist Rosemary Righter criticized the thinking of 'the affluent children of the prosperous West' who demonstrated against capitalism although it was 'good, not bad' for the world's poor:

'These are highly diverse groups... but what they have in common is detestation of... capitalism, multinational corporations, free capital markets.... The poor they say must be "protected" from these forces – protected, that is, from the things that have made their own societies rich.'

always as low as they can possibly be. Capitalism is closely linked to globalization as the breaking down of barriers to trade across countries means that producers of goods have the whole world as their market. This is known as global capitalism. The protest movement believed that more restrictions or controls were needed on the activities of the multinational businesses that dominated the world economy, and on big investors shifting millions of dollars around the globe.

Anti-capitalism – the desire to resist, reform, or overthrow global capitalism – is not just a recent development; it has a long history. This book will look at the early forms of protest that modern capitalism provoked, and at the development of the idea of **socialism** as a fully-fledged alternative to capitalism. It will examine why the socialist alternative for a long time seemed so attractive to so many people, but also why, by the 1990s, it was widely thought to have failed. It will look at the current protest movement and explain its place in a long tradition of violent and non-violent action against established authority. And it will discuss what realistic contribution the 'anti-capitalist' movement might make to the future of the world in the twenty-first century.

An anti-capitalist protester wearing a jester's hat and a gas mask demonstrates near the site of the Summit of the Americas in Quebec City, Canada, 22 April 2001.

The Rise of Capitalism

The rise of modern global **capitalism** can be traced back to the start of the Industrial Revolution in Western countries. This great change was first evident in Britain. From around 1780, enterprising British businessmen began to invest in new machinery powered by steam or water. The use of these machines, operated by workers in large-scale factories, allowed Britain's production of cotton goods to multiply fifty-fold between 1785 and 1850.

The output of other industries such as pottery-making and iron-founding also grew steeply, as did production from coal mines. This Industrial Revolution was linked to changing attitudes to business. The idea spread that allowing businessmen to pursue profit and trade without restrictions or interference from government (that is, in a 'free market') was the best way to increase national wealth. The combination of business enterprise with the use of machines in factories is sometimes called 'industrial capitalism'.

Luddites

In 1811 skilled workers in the English counties of Nottinghamshire, Lancashire and Yorkshire began destroying newly introduced textile machinery. Known as 'Luddites', they rightly feared that the machines would destroy their livelihood by making goods faster and cheaper than they could manage on their hand looms. The movement continued for several years but was eventually ruthlessly suppressed by the authorities. Many Luddites were hanged or deported to Australia. 'Luddite' has since become a term used for anyone who opposes the introduction of new technology.

In the nineteenth century new machinery – here the first steam hammer, 1842 – rapidly increased output of manufactured goods, making fortunes for capitalist factory owners.

Economic growth

Industrialization at first affected only a small minority of the population, even in Britain. But during the course of the nineteenth century, industrial capitalism generated huge economic growth. The money made from producing goods more quickly and cheaply was spent on building more factories and mines and constructing more new machinery. There seemed to be no limit to the expanding production and technological innovation, or to the money being made from both. Parts of Europe and the United States followed in Britain's wake, chasing and in many cases overtaking the British in industrial output. By 1914, people were producing some fifty times more goods and services worldwide than they had in the 1780s. Most of this extra production was in Western Europe and North America.

Unhealthy conditions

Despite its ability to generate such vast wealth, the rise of industrial capitalism initially had a grim effect on the lives of working people. Many craftsmen lost their livelihood as new machinery replaced their skills with simple repetitive tasks, often carried out by unskilled women and children who were cheaper to employ. Conditions in factories and mines were usually terrible. Workers were made to work excessively long hours for low wages in an environment that was unhealthy and often downright dangerous. There was nothing new about poverty or hard work. But in the first half of the nineteenth century, the sight of the filthy, insanitary new industrial towns such as Manchester in northern England shocked everyone who visited them.

During the Industrial Revolution, working people laboured for long hours in bad conditions for low pay. Here children haul coal in a mine shaft in Britain in the 1840s.

At the same time, traditional forms of support and protection for working people and the poor were swept aside as being against the spirit of capitalism. Enterprising people were encouraged to make their fortunes, but the less fortunate were left to fend for themselves. Traditional forms of charity for the poor in time of need were denounced by the supporters of capitalism as undermining the will to work. Previously many skilled workers had belonged to guilds, organizations that protected their interests and guaranteed them employment, while also fixing wages and prices. Now guilds were abolished. Workers were 'free' to sell their labour to whoever would employ them for whatever wage they could get. They could also be laid off by employers whenever they were no longer needed.

Child labour in the USA

Although in the nineteenth century many European countries passed laws limiting or banning the use of child labour in factories and mines, in the United States capitalists remained free to **exploit** children as cheap workers. Around 1900 it was common, for example, for the children of newly arrived immigrants in New York to work for up to sixteen hours a day in dangerous, disease-ridden factories. These factories were known as 'sweatshops' because the work there was so hard.

Workers' revolt

With their livelihoods threatened, some workers resisted in the most direct way by machine-breaking.

Direct action: Luddites smash textile machinery.

Tolpuddle Martyrs

In the nineteenth century, many workers who reacted to capitalism by forming **trade unions** faced harsh persecution. In 1834 six farm labourers from the village of Tolpuddle in Dorset, south-west England, were transported (that is, exiled as criminals) to Australia for forming a union to resist a cut in their wages. Their harsh sentence provoked a national outcry and they were freed two years later. On his return, one of the 'martyrs', George Loveless, called on workers to join together to defend their rights: 'Let every working man come forward,' he wrote, 'from east to west, and from north to south, unite firmly but peaceably together as the heart of one man.'

This happened both in towns and in the countryside – for example, British farm workers wrecked agricultural machinery in the 1830s. Some workers tried to form trade unions to defend their interests, fighting for higher wages and recognition of craft skills. But trade unions long remained illegal and faced brutal repression by the authorities.

Reform

Over time, criticism of the poor working conditions that industrial capitalism produced and fear of a workers' revolt led to a steady trickle of reforms. In many European countries, governments intervened to ban child labour and limit working hours in factories and mines.

By 1914, the introduction of state pensions and unemployment insurance had begun to soften the harshness of working–class life, especially in Germany and Britain. Factory workers also began to share modestly in rising wealth and became consumers of the new cheap goods that industry produced. Much of the ordinary working population of Western Europe and North America was, by 1914, far better off than a century before – although inequality between rich and poor remained huge.

Effect on the rest of the world

The impact of industrial capitalism, from the very start, was felt on a worldwide scale. The booming British textile industry imported raw cotton from abroad – causing, for instance, a huge expansion in slave-worked cotton plantations in the southern United States in the early nineteenth century. And a large proportion of the products of the British cotton mills were sold abroad. India, once a place that produced textiles for export to Europe, had by 1850 become a large-scale importer of cotton goods made in Lancashire.

Countries could not choose to stay outside the new global economy dominated by the industrializing West. The Industrial Revolution gave the Western powers weapons far superior to any elsewhere in the world, from machine-guns to iron steam-powered gunboats. The so-called Opium Wars (1839-42 and 1856-60) made the proud Chinese Empire open its doors to foreign trade. Japan, where the *shoguns* (local rulers) exercised tight control on trade with the outside world, was threatened by a fleet of US warships commanded by Commodore Perry in

The Opium Wars

In the early nineteenth century, British merchants were determined to open up trade with China. They had two problems: the Chinese authorities wanted to keep foreign trade under strict control, and the Chinese did not want any of the goods the British had to sell. The British eventually found a product that the Chinese consumers would buy – the drug opium, produced from poppies in British-ruled India. Understandably, the Chinese authorities did not want their people to become drug addicts and tried to stop the opium trade. In 1839 the British responded by waging war on China. Defeated, the Chinese were forced to open ports to British trade. A further war in 1856, in which Britain was aided by France, forced China to abandon all attempts to exclude foreign goods or investment. China became an open field for European and North American capitalists to exploit at will.

1853-4 and forced to begin opening its ports. In many places Europeans seized direct control of territory which became a part of worldwide empires. Most of Africa, India, and Southeast Asia was under European rule by 1900.

Following the West

Given the overwhelming economic and military success of Western Europe and North America, those countries that could tried to imitate them,

During the first Opium War, Britain's Royal Navy destroyed the warships of the Chinese Empire with superior guns produced by the factories of the Industrial Revolution.

developing their own industries and adopting Westernized styles of government and society. Japan was the most successful at this, and from 1868 onwards created its own industrial revolution. But the West did not favour industrial development in Asia, South America or Africa. Western investment created new ports, roads and railways in these regions to exploit previously untouched mineral resources and develop agricultural production. But this was so that these regions could supply cheap raw materials to, and buy manufactured products from, factories in Europe and North America. The West did not intend that these countries should compete with it.

By 1914 global capitalism was generating huge profits for investors, businessmen and financiers in Europe and North America. It was also generating enough wealth to give benefits and new opportunities to ordinary working people in these industrial heartlands. But at the same time it faced a large-scale movement that took an alternative view of the future, and hoped and expected to replace capitalist civilization with something more just and more efficient – **socialism**.

Conservative anti-capitalists

Much of the early opposition to the rise of the new industrial capitalists and their way of doing business came from conservatives – people who wanted society to stay the same or turn backwards. This feeling was especially strong among rural landowners, who had traditionally enjoyed a dominant position in society. Conservatives argued that life had been better for working people when they had been tied to the land, serving a local lord or squire all their lives. This was preferable, they claimed, to being capitalist 'free labour' – which meant taking whatever job they could find, or enduring spells of unemployment. Even slave owners in the southern United States used this argument, claiming their slaves were more secure and better cared-for than 'free' factory workers in the northern USA. Very few slaves seem to have agreed with their owners on this point.

The Alternative Vision

Socialism first appeared in the early nineteenth century. This was a time when the idea of political equality – that all people should have the same rights, such as the right to vote – was winning increasing acceptance. Socialists extended the idea of equality to social and economic life. They argued that political equality was meaningless if most people were living in poverty in a society dominated by a minority of the rich.

Throughout the nineteenth century, the right to vote was extended to people in many countries. Here voting takes place in Cheyenne, Wyoming, the first US state to give women the vote.

A better world?

Early socialists (often called '**utopian socialists**') put forward idealistic projects to create a kinder, better world. They envisaged a society based on harmony and cooperation rather than on competition and greed. **Capitalism** saw society as made up of individuals pursuing their personal advantage and satisfaction. But, socialists argued, the success of enterprising capitalists was often at other people's expense. If society was run differently, they said, people could live peacefully in communities where wealth was shared equally, and necessary work was performed cheerfully and without compulsion. This would be an egalitarian society – one in which no one had more money or property than anyone else.

Visions of Utopia

In 1891 Irish author Oscar Wilde, a supporter of socialism in the late nineteenth century, argued that humanity needed visions of an ideal society, or 'Utopia', to aim at, even if they might seem unrealistic:

'A map of the world that does not include Utopia is not worth even glancing at, for it leaves out the one country at which Humanity is always landing. And when Humanity lands there, it looks out, and, seeing a better country, sets sail. Progress is the realization of Utopias.'

British socialist Robert Owen founded his industrial community at New Harmony in Indiana, USA in 1825. Owen hoped it would be a model for a future society based on equality and cooperation.

Self-governing communities

Two early leading socialists were Robert Owen in Britain and Charles Fourier in France. Owen, who rose from being a draper's assistant to become a wealthy cotton-mill owner, created an industrial community at New Lanark in Scotland that he hoped would point the way to a better society. Around two thousand workers were housed in clean, identical living quarters with facilities that included a concert hall and a lecture theatre. Owen went on to establish a self-governing egalitarian community at New Harmony in Indiana, USA, in 1825.

This bold experiment in communal living was not a permanent success. Nor were similar **communes** set up by Fourier's followers in the 1830s, also in the United States (chosen because there was plenty of land and the authorities were less likely to interfere). In truth, these early socialists were often far from realistic. Fourier, for example, argued that all the most dirty and disgusting jobs in society could be done by small children, since children have a natural love of dirt! Above all, they had little idea of how to move from the existing society to a future egalitarian socialist society. Their plans simply required people to have a sudden change of heart.

Cooperative movements

Many working people and small producers in the nineteenth century were drawn to setting up 'cooperatives'. These businesses were run cooperatively for the equal benefit of all involved not, as in the capitalist economy, for the competitive, profit-making interests of a handful of owners. In Britain, for example, twenty-eight Lancashire working men opened a cooperative shop in Toad Lane, Rochdale, in 1844. From these humble beginnings British cooperative stores grew into a nationwide movement. Regular 'co-op' shoppers became, in effect, **shareholders** in their stores. In other countries producers' cooperatives were more important, with large numbers of small farmers joining together to market their produce. In Denmark, for example, by 1892 there were more than one thousand cooperative dairies. Most Danish bacon, eggs, milk and fruit was produced and marketed cooperatively. Both cooperative stores and producers' cooperatives have continued to flourish up to the present day in many parts of the world, including the United States.

17

Karl Marx, left, and Friedrich Engels were lifelong collaborators in the struggle to overthrow capitalism.

Class conflict

Socialism only became a major force when its ideas began to relate to social and political conflict in the nineteenth century. The person largely responsible for making this link was the German thinker and **political activist** Karl Marx. For Marx, the key to understanding what was happening in the world lay in what he called '**class conflict**'. If a socialist society was going to come about, he argued, it would be through a revolt of the mass of factory workers – the working class or '**proletariat**'.

At the time, according to Marx, society was ruled by the '**bourgeoisie**' – industrialists, financiers and property owners – who robbed the workers by paying them much less for their work than the things they produced were worth. But, said Marx, the workers would one day rise up against **bourgeois rule** and take power for themselves. This revolution or class conflict would result in a workers'

Workers unite!

From early on, the struggle for socialism was seen as a global struggle, which workers should join in regardless of nationality. Karl Marx's *Communist Manifesto* of 1848 concluded with a famous call to action:

'*The workers have nothing to lose but their chains. They have a world to win. Workers of the world, unite!*'

government, that would take factories and businesses away from their owners and run them for the benefit of the workers, ending the system of labour for private profit. This would lead eventually to 'communism', a state of perfect equality, freedom and self-fulfilment for all.

The overthrow of capitalism

Marx's vision, worked out in his writings over many years, became massively influential. His work established the idea that capitalism was the cause of the world's woes and that the overthrow of capitalism was the way forward for humanity. Marx did not, however, want to turn the clock back to before the industrial age. He believed that industrialization made a future equal society possible, as enough goods could be produced for everyone, and no one need be poor. His vision seemed to show that the overthrow of capitalism was not just desirable, but inevitable – the necessary next stage in the evolution of human society.

Marx's view of the industrial working class as the people who would start a socialist revolution made sense, since they were growing in numbers and, in many cases, were angry about the conditions in which they lived and worked. Workers were naturally drawn to coming together to try to improve their lives, since individually they had no power and few opportunities.

Karl Marx

Born in Trier, Germany, Karl Marx (1818-83) spent most of his life in London because, as a political activist, he would have been arrested in mainland Europe. With his lifelong associate Friedrich Engels, he wrote and organized tirelessly to undermine the capitalist system. His *Communist Manifesto*, a rousing call for a worldwide workers' revolution, appeared in 1848 and the first volume of his massive analysis of the capitalist system, *Das Kapital* (Capital), followed in 1867. Marx was more successful as a writer than in practical politics. The First International Working Men's Association, which he helped to set up in 1864 to organize socialists from different countries into a single movement, fell apart amid bitter divisions in 1872. Although Marx was unwavering in his absolute opposition to capitalism, his ideas varied over time. After his death, some of his thoughts were shaped into a rigid way of thinking, Marxism. It has been correctly said that Marx was not himself a **Marxist**.

Workers' struggle

Trade unions became one of the most characteristic features of industrial society, grouping workers together in a collective struggle against their employers for better pay and conditions. The socialist argument that employers were idle parasites living off the sweat of the workers corresponded to most working people's view of their own situation.

The capitalist system, however, proved far tougher than its enemies first believed. When Marx published his *Communist Manifesto* in 1848, he was convinced that capitalism was on its last legs. But a spate of revolutionary uprisings across Europe in that year – in which socialists of various kinds played a limited but significant part – were put down without achieving any fundamental social change. Further popular uprisings in Paris in 1871, in Russia in 1905, and in Barcelona in 1909 were equally unsuccessful.

Socialist programmes

Although the expected revolution to replace capitalism by a new kind of society did not come, socialist movements grew to be a major influence in Europe (much less so in the USA). In countries such as Britain, France and Germany, political parties with

Protesters on the march during the failed revolutionary uprising in Russia in 1905. Their banners include one repeating Marx's slogan: 'Workers of the world, unite!'

socialist programmes – ranging from 'minimum' demands such as for a legal limit on working time to eight hours a day to 'maximum' aims for the eventual takeover of all large businesses by the state – won the majority of working-class votes.

Such parties, like the trade unions to which they were linked, were distinctly 'anti-capitalist' in blaming the world's ills, especially the existence of poverty and inequality, on financiers and industrialists. But in day-to-day political life they concentrated on promoting gradual reforms, for example winning reductions in working hours. This reflected the basic concerns of most of their working-class supporters. Inevitably, there were groups of revolutionary **extremists**, notably **anarchists**, who opposed this gradual reform and called for absolute opposition to capitalism and the ruling classes.

A demonstration by trade unionists in Manchester in 1874: the unions expressed the workers' sense of solidarity in opposition to their employers.

Anarchism

Anarchism is a type of socialism that developed in the nineteenth century, mostly through the influence of French thinker Pierre Joseph Proudhon (1809-65) and Russian activist Mikhail Bakunin (1814-76). Hostile to government of any kind, anarchists believed that small-scale self-governing communities would be the building blocks of a new society. They rejected taking part in parliamentary elections or in negotiations to improve workers' conditions. Instead many of them recommended 'direct action' against governments and capitalists. In practice this meant the assassination of political leaders by terrorists and **militant** strike action by anarchist trade unionists, known as '**anarcho-syndicalists**'. Although their ideal was a world of perfect peace and harmony, many anarchists believed violence was essential to shake the foundations of the capitalist order. Bakunin declared that 'the passion for destruction is at the same time a creative passion.'

Violent gestures

Through the late nineteenth and early twentieth centuries there were many terrorist attacks, including assassinations of political leaders, mostly carried out by anarchists. One of the victims was US President William McKinley, shot dead by anarchist Leon Czolgosz in 1901. Anarchists described such actions as '**propaganda** by the deed', violent gestures that would draw attention to the injustice and oppression in the world.

Although condemning such extremism, more mainstream socialists did not accept that their role was simply to improve the workers' lot within capitalist society. The German Social Democrat Party adopted Marxism as its **ideology**, while the British Labour Party did not. But both at least in theory looked forward to the day when the capitalist system would be replaced with a socialist alternative. Socialist parties were reluctant to consider compromising their principles by taking part in running a capitalist state, although the Social Democrats in Denmark broke ranks to take a share in government from 1913.

The anarchist Leon Czolgosz assassinates the president of the United States, William McKinley, on 6 September 1901.

Industrial Workers of the World

Probably the most impressive anti-capitalist organization ever created in the United States was the Industrial Workers of the World (IWW), founded in Chicago in 1905. This was an anarcho-syndicalist movement dedicated to using **labor union** action to confront and ultimately overthrow capitalist society. The IWW organized a series of major strikes during which workers engaged in direct action against employers – one of its slogans was 'negotiate with dynamite'. It hoped one day for a 'general strike' of all workers to bring about the downfall of capitalism. The IWW grew to have around 100,000 members. When the United States entered the First World War in 1917, however, the IWW, which opposed the war, was crushed by the authorities. Its organization was broken up and many of its activists jailed.

Emma Goldman

Emma Goldman was one of the most prominent American anarchists of her day. Born in Lithuania in 1869, she emigrated to the USA when she was sixteen. There she met her lifelong companion, Alexander Berkman, and became involved in anarchist politics. In 1892 Goldman and Berkman planned revenge on Pennsylvania steel company chairman Henry Clay Frick, who had used armed police to shoot striking workers. Berkman shot and stabbed Frick, but failed to kill him, and was imprisoned for fourteen years. An inspired public speaker, Goldman continued to advocate such acts of violence against the rich and powerful. After assassinating President McKinley in 1901, anarchist Leon Czolgosz described himself as 'a disciple of Emma Goldman – her words set me on fire.' Goldman herself was repeatedly imprisoned and eventually, in 1919, deported from the United States to Russia and deprived of her citizenship. She hated the communist regime in Russia and later renounced her belief in acts of violence. But up to her death in 1940 she never lost her faith in the possibility of creating a freer world by the overthrow of existing capitalist society. She was also a leading campaigner for women's rights.

May Day

So, by 1914, in the European heartlands of industrial capitalism, **mass movements** existed that were dedicated, at least in theory, to overthrowing the capitalist system. From 1890, May Day was established as an annual socialist festival. And every year on this day millions of workers in different countries marched under red banners, the symbol of socialism. In 1889 the Second International was set up. This was an organization that brought together socialist parties from different countries, arguing that workers had common interests that went beyond national boundaries. Socialists confidently expected that one day the workers would inherit the Earth. But what actually happened next – the First World War – was a shock to both the capitalist system and its enemies.

Anarchist Emma Goldman.

Communism and Social Democracy

During the twentieth century, the only practical attempt to create and run an alternative to **capitalism** was made by the countries that adopted communism. Another emerging trend saw **social democrats** in charge of the governments of capitalist states running capitalist economies.

The First World War (1914–18) brought all the major industrial countries into conflict. The vast resources of industrial capitalism were devoted to the work of the war, which led to the deaths of around ten million people. The war was a disaster for the capitalist system, creating political and economic instability that would last for decades. But it was also, in its way, a disaster for international **socialism**.

Before 1914, socialists had claimed that workers across the world had more in common with one

Vladimir Ilyich Lenin

When Lenin (1870-1924) was an adolescent, his elder brother was executed for his part in a plot to assassinate Tsar Alexander III. Lenin in his turn became a revolutionary activist, adopting Marxism and helping found a Russian Social Democrat party. In 1903 he caused a split in the Social Democrats which left him as leader of the hardline Bolshevik faction. Lenin was living in exile in Switzerland when the Tsarist government in Russia was overthrown in February 1917. He returned to Russia and led the Bolsheviks to seize power in November 1917. Lenin refused to allow other socialist groups any share in the new government. He believed that the only way to make a successful revolution was through the leadership of a disciplined revolutionary party. In practice this meant that his communist state became a single-party dictatorship, without **democracy** or respect for individual freedom.

another than with governments or employers in their own countries. However, workers flocked to fight for their country during the First World War, and most socialists supported their homeland. Only a small minority of socialists called for workers to shun the 'capitalist war'. One of these was the exiled leader of the Russian Bolshevik Party, Vladimir Ilyich Lenin, who saw the conflict as an opportunity at last to overthrow the capitalist system.

The October Revolution

As the war dragged on, with mounting casualties, initial enthusiasm evaporated and social conflicts surfaced once more. In February 1917, the **Tsarist regime** in Russia collapsed in the face of popular discontent. Lenin returned from exile and, that October, led the Bolsheviks – soon renamed 'communists' – to seize power and proclaim a workers' state. Lenin's hope and expectation was that revolutionary socialists in other countries, especially Germany, would also take power. But despite widespread upheavals at the end of the war and some shortlived attempts to found workers' states – for example, in Hungary and the German state of

Bavaria – Russia was the only place in which a revolutionary government survived. In the absence of revolution elsewhere in the world, the Russian communists adopted the policy of 'building socialism in a single country'.

In 1917, armed workers, soldiers and sailors gave Lenin's Bolsheviks the firepower to seize control of Russia.

The survival of Lenin's communist regime was achieved through an utterly ruthless suppression of all opposition. The communists did not hesitate to shoot workers who protested at the regime's policies. In 1923 the Union of Soviet Socialist Republics (USSR or Soviet Union) was formally founded, ruling most of the old territory of the Russian empire. It was a state in which all power was in the hands of a single organization, the Communist Party.

Social democrats

The revolution in Russia split the international socialist movement in two. Communist parties aligned with the Soviet Union opposed socialist parties that believed in democracy and individual freedom (social democrats). The social democrats shifted away from the idea of an overthrow of the capitalist system. Instead, they wanted state control of only certain key areas of the economy – typically central banks, transport, and the largest industries – and measures to make the distribution of wealth in society fairer, for example by heavier taxation of the rich. Social democratic parties began to form governments. The Labour Party, for example, held power in Britain for the first time in 1924 – without in any way overturning the basic order of society.

Communists

The communist parties, on the other hand, were committed to the overthrow of capitalism and of liberal democracy – the form of government most associated with free-market capitalism, involving the election of governments and parliaments and respect for individual human rights. The communist parties formed part of an organization, the Third International, based in Moscow. In practice, their policies were dictated by the Soviet Union and often designed to serve Soviet interests. Communist activists accepted this, because they saw the survival

During the Great Depression of the early 1930s, unemployed American workers were reduced to queueing for handouts of free food. While millions of people went hungry, food produce from farms rotted unsold, because the unemployed had no money to buy it with.

of the Soviet Union as an essential first step towards what would eventually be a world revolution.

The idea of a worldwide collapse of capitalism was far more believable in the 1920s and 1930s than it had been before the First World War. Global capitalism pre-1914 was an immensely well-organized, coordinated system, with a large measure of **free trade** and financial stability. The attempt to recreate this system in the 1920s failed and, by 1930, the world was plunged in the Great Depression (see box), with mass unemployment and a catastrophic drop in world trade. Indeed, in the 1930s the free movement of goods and money around the world effectively ceased.

The Great Depression

The Great Depression was a worldwide economic slump in the early 1930s. It was triggered, at least in the United States, by the great **stock market** crash of 1929. The Depression brought mass unemployment and poverty to much of the world. Critics of capitalism saw the Great Depression as a clear example of the madness of the capitalist system. The stock market crash, they felt, showed the harmful effects of financial speculation, which made the fate of nations turn on what was, in effect, no more than a gambling casino.

The rise of fascism

The Depression created a widespread feeling that capitalism had failed and was on the wane. Liberal democracy was also apparently in decline. Some countries in Western Europe became **right-wing** dictatorships, notably Italy, ruled by Benito Mussolini's Fascist Party, and Germany, ruled by Adolf Hitler's Nazi Party. Mussolini and Hitler opposed communism and socialism (communists and socialists were put in concentration camps in Nazi Germany) and they had the support of most large corporations in their countries. But the dictators did not believe in free-market capitalism. They made capitalist businesses serve their goal of building up national economic and military power, rather than pursuing profit any way they wished.

Even in the USA, where the stock market crash of 1929 was followed by mass unemployment, President Franklin D. Roosevelt's New Deal, although not socialist, was far removed from the traditional American belief in free enterprise. Under the New Deal of 1933, the government strove to provide work for the unemployed, give social security to the poor, and support the activities of **labor unions**.

German dictator Adolf Hitler attends a military review during the rapid rearmament of Germany in the 1930s.

The Soviet model

With capitalism apparently in disarray, it is hardly surprising that many people in the capitalist West were fascinated by the attempt to build a 'socialist alternative' in the Soviet Union. During the 1920s in the Soviet Union there was a large measure of state control and planning, but there was also some small-scale free enterprise. The latter existed especially in the countryside, where peasants kept the land they had seized during the revolution. From 1929, under the **dictatorial** rule of Josef Stalin, this changed. The Soviet Union embarked on rapid industrialization, in which the state laid down production targets for each industry and assigned investment, labour and materials as it thought appropriate. Agriculture was 'collectivized' – meaning that the land was taken from the peasants to create large state-owned farms.

Leon Trotsky

Trotsky (original name Lev Davidovich Bronstein) was second only to Lenin as leader of the Russian Revolution. After Lenin's death in 1924, however, Trotsky lost out in a power struggle with Stalin and was expelled from the Soviet Union in 1929. Trotsky argued that Stalin had betrayed the cause of international socialism, instead putting socialism at the service of his own dictatorship. He called for a 'permanent revolution' that would stop oppressive **bureaucrats** taking over the revolution, as he argued had happened in the Soviet Union. In 1940 Trotsky was murdered in Mexico by one of Stalin's agents. Trotskyism attracted those who held a traditional **Marxist** belief in a revolution based on the industrial working class, but who disliked Soviet-style communism.

Revolutionary Leon Trotsky.

Official Soviet photos of the 1930s showed well-fed Ukrainian peasants enjoying life on new collective farms. In reality, the peasants endured brutal repression and mass starvation.

In the 1930s, as industry in the capitalist world stagnated or declined, Soviet industry expanded fast. But the human cost was terrible. The collectivization policy led to mass starvation, especially in the Ukraine, killing millions of people. Millions of other Soviet citizens became political prisoners and were used as slave labour. Stalin turned the communist state into a personal dictatorship. Many thousands of dedicated communist activists, including most of the leaders of the 1917 revolution, were 'purged' (killed or imprisoned) as Stalin rid himself of any possible opposition.

Yet many people, even inside the Soviet Union, continued to believe that this was merely the necessary cost of building a better future. In the West, communist sympathizers refused to believe reports of the horrors of Soviet life that appeared in the 'bourgeois' press. Instead they believed ludicrously optimistic accounts of Soviet life written by people who supported the communist cause.

Anti-colonialism

The example of Soviet communism inspired many of those in the developing world who wanted to liberate their countries from Western domination. Communists argued that China and India, Africa and the West Indies could only ever be truly independent of the West if they withdrew from the capitalist system. Otherwise, even if they had their own governments, they would still suffer from economic exploitation by Western business interests. In their

Gandhi and civil disobedience

The most prominent anti-colonialist leader of the 1920s and 1930s was the Indian nationalist Mohandas 'Mahatma' Gandhi (1869-1948). Gandhi's greatest innovation in his campaign to end British rule in India was the use of **civil disobedience** as a form of protest and resistance. Protesters practising civil disobedience were prepared to obstruct the authorities and deliberately break laws with which they disagreed, but were strictly non-violent, even if attacked or arrested. Gandhi's example of non-violent resistance has been used by many other protest movements, including anti-capitalist ones, up to the present day.

view, anti-colonialism and anti-capitalism were inextricably linked, because all the **colonial powers** were capitalist. The leaders of anti-colonial movements in the 1930s included the communist Ho Chi Minh in Vietnam (then part of French Indochina). Many non-communist anti-colonialists, such as Jawaharlal Nehru in India, were strongly influenced by socialist ideas.

The power and political standing of the Soviet Union were massively increased by its successes during the Second World War, when it played a leading role in defeating Nazi Germany. This victory allowed the Soviet Union to set up communist regimes in Poland, Hungary, Czechoslovakia, Romania, Bulgaria,

Mao Tse-tung

Chinese communist leader Mao Tse-tung (1893-1976) drew support mainly from peasants in the countryside rather than industrial workers in the cities. He won power in 1949 after building a peasant army to fight a **guerrilla** war against China's nationalist rulers. This led Mao to state that: 'Political power grows out of the barrel of a gun.' Like Lenin in Russia, Mao established a single-party dictatorship in China. In the 1960s he turned against the Soviet Union, denouncing Soviet leaders for deserting true socialism. In 1966 he encouraged the Cultural Revolution, an uprising by young **extremists** in China against teachers, civil servants, and many other authority figures. Mao was an attractive figure to many Western radicals in the 1960s, and some Western students called themselves 'Maoists'. But since his death there have been many revelations of the brutality, oppression and corruption of his regime.

Chinese revolutionary and dictator Mao Tse-tung.

East Germany, and North Korea. In 1949 China, the world's most populous country, came under communist rule. At this point a great swathe of the world stretching from the Pacific to central Europe was under communist control.

The Cold War

From the late 1940s to the late 1980s, the Soviet Union faced capitalist North America and Western Europe in a confrontation known as the Cold War. The United States – by 1945 by far the most powerful country in the West – dedicated itself to preventing communism spreading any further. It argued that it was protecting the 'free world'. Social democrat parties placed themselves solidly on the American side in the Cold War, confirming their commitment to democracy and individual freedom.

Soviet tanks on the streets of Budapest during the crushing of the Hungarian uprising in October 1956.

During the 1950s many people in the West who had previously been communists or sympathized with the Soviet Union sharply altered their views. One reason was Soviet behaviour in Eastern Europe. Communist governments were imposed on countries such as Poland, Czechoslovakia and Hungary and all opposition was brutally suppressed. In 1956, when Hungarians rebelled against communist rule, the Soviet Union sent in tanks to crush the uprising. In the same year, Stalin's successor as Soviet leader, Nikita Khrushchev, publicly admitted to some of the horrors of Stalin's rule. Many former sympathizers reluctantly accepted that Soviet communism was a force for oppression, not liberation.

Yet the threat to capitalism from Soviet-style communism seemed very real. This was not just because of the military power of the Soviet Union. The Soviets had proved that a different way of running a modern economy – through state control, state ownership and state planning – could be made to work. Communist parties even enjoyed popular support in some Western European democracies, notably France and Italy. Khrushchev once claimed that 'socialism would bury capitalism'. It did not seem an impossible future.

French communists demonstrate in Paris in 1947. The Communist Party was a significant force in French politics up to the 1990s.

The Third World and the New Left

The anti-capitalist protests we see today grew directly out of radical movements of the 1950s and 1960s. This was a time of resistance to Western **capitalism** in parts of Africa, Asia and South America, and of political protest in Europe and North America, especially among young people. The young protesters of the 1960s in particular invented styles of political action that have continued to the present day.

In the second half of the twentieth century, it became customary to talk of the globe as divided into three: the First World of the highly developed Western capitalist countries and Japan; the Second World of the communist countries, stretching from Eastern Europe to the Pacific; and the Third World, made up of Africa, Latin America, and much of Asia. The mass of the population of the Third World lived in extreme poverty, and many Third World countries were under colonial rule. Not surprisingly, the Third World became an area where revolutionary activity and socialist ideas gathered force.

Multinational companies based in the developed world have been blamed for devastating forests in developing countries. Here, a dirt road cuts into the remote rainforest in Borneo to provide access for logging vehicles.

National independence

To begin with, much of the attention was focused on achieving national independence. Between 1947 and the mid-1970s most countries were freed from colonial rule, some peacefully and some only after prolonged armed struggles against the **colonial powers**. But it was clear that political independence in itself would not solve the problems of poverty and **underdevelopment**, or put the newly independent countries on an equal footing with their former

colonial masters. They were still powerless in the face
of the capitalist system. They had to turn to the
former colonial powers for investment and technology,
and sell their goods in a world market controlled by
big businesses and financiers located in the West.
Looking for a way forward, many leaders in the Third
World took the Soviet Union or China as their model
and adopted socialist economic policies. Almost all
believed in the pursuit of rapid industrialization as the
only path to economic development.

American involvement

From the 1950s onwards the United States became
determined to limit the spread of communism.
It was actively involved in either supporting or
opposing Third World governments, depending on
whether they seemed to be for or against the
capitalist West. Many governments supported by the
United States were **undemocratic**, corrupt, denied
their people essential human rights and used methods
such as torture against their opponents. This was
especially true in Latin America, where various
left-wing revolutionary **guerrilla** and terrorist
groups took on American-backed **military regimes**
in the 1960s and 1970s.

In 1973 Chilean army
leader General Pinochet
(left) overthrew the
democratically elected
government of President
Salvador Allende (right).

In Chile in 1973 the United States
even backed a **military coup** to
overthrow a democratically elected
left-wing government. Americans
may have seen this as defending
the 'free world' against communist
oppression, but to many of the
world's poorest people the United
States simply appeared to be bent
on keeping them in poverty so
that American business interests
(and thereby global capitalism)
could flourish.

Communism takes root

Two places in which communism was successfully established were the island of Cuba in the Caribbean and Vietnam in Southeast Asia. In Cuba, Fidel Castro came to power at the end of 1958 after fighting a guerrilla war against a **right-wing** dictatorship. Castro declared his country communist and formed close links with the Soviet Union. The United States imposed a **trade blockade** on Cuba, backed an invasion of the island by Cuban exiles in 1961, and attempted to assassinate Castro, but the communist regime, and its leader, survived.

In the 1960s the United States became heavily involved in the defence of capitalist South Vietnam against a guerrilla uprising backed by communist-ruled North Vietnam. Despite a massive commitment of military power – some 50,000 American soldiers died in the conflict – the United States was unable to achieve its objectives. In 1975, two years after the withdrawal of American forces, South Vietnam and its neighbours Cambodia and Laos all came under communist control.

The deployment of American soldiers in Vietnam failed to stop the spread of communism in Southeast Asia.

Radical movements in the West

It was not surprising that revolutionary **socialism** and communism should have flourished in the poverty-stricken Third World. But it was startling that the 1960s and 1970s should have

Overthrowing Western society

In 1967 Stokely Carmichael, a Black Power activist in the United States, declared his support for the oppressed of the Third World:

*'Our enemy is white Western **imperialist** society.... Our struggle is to overthrow this system which feeds itself and expands itself through the economic and cultural exploitation of non-white, non-Western peoples – the Third World.'*

brought a wave of radical and revolutionary movements to North America, Western Europe and Japan. These were areas enjoying prosperity on an unprecedented scale. Rapid economic growth, generally combined with greater equality, meant that most of the population was strikingly better off than ever before. Average industrial workers' wages doubled in Western Europe between 1950 and 1965. Most people not only had new possessions – television sets, family cars, washing machines, fridges – but also better food and health care, better education and housing.

This prosperity was provided by capitalism, although not unbridled capitalism. That is to say, governments exercised tight controls on the movement of money across their borders, for example. They also often intervened in the working of the economy to avoid any return to the mass unemployment of the Great Depression. Most countries in Western Europe had what was called a 'mixed economy', with some major industries under state control, as in a socialist system, but the overall economy working on free-market capitalist principles.

Che Guevara (on extreme left of photo) and Fidel Castro (standing) in the mountains of the Sierra Maestra during the guerrilla campaign in Cuba in the 1950s.

Ernesto 'Che' Guevara

Argentinian-born revolutionary Ernesto 'Che' Guevara (1928-67) was a hero to thousands of radical students in the 1960s. After fighting alongside Fidel Castro in the guerrilla war that brought a revolutionary government to power in Cuba in 1959, Guevara embarked on a personal mission to encourage guerrilla uprisings in other Third World countries, among poor peasants whom he regarded as victims of capitalist exploitation. He believed that faced with 'many Vietnams', the United States, the leader of the capitalist world, would be overstretched and encircled by revolutionary states. Guevara was killed in Bolivia in 1967 after his small group of guerrillas was ambushed by government forces.

Most countries also had some form of welfare state, with publicly funded health and education services, council housing, social security and state pensions providing support 'from the cradle to the grave'. Taxation was widely used to redistribute wealth from the rich to the poor, especially in countries where **social democrat** parties were in power all or part of the time – as in Sweden and Britain.

Youth culture

Yet amid this growing prosperity a new wave of anti-capitalism and radical protest gathered strength, especially among young people, present in society in especially large numbers because of the post-Second World War 'baby boom'. The youth culture, centred on rock/pop music, that emerged in the late 1950s and 1960s, was instinctively anti-authority – against teachers, parents, 'old' people generally (a famous saying of the time was 'never trust anyone over 30'). The growing prosperity and increasing opportunities brought by an expanding economy tended to make the young scornful of the cautious, narrow views of their elders. The more idealistic young people sensed that they could make a better world than the old men who ruled the world – in 1960 the political leaders of the United States, Germany, France and Britain were respectively 70, 84, 70 and 66 years old.

There were plenty of causes for protest. In the United States racism was rife, with African Americans in the Southern states denied the most basic civil rights. Many students, both black and white, had their

Consumer action

In 1965, American Ralph Nader published *Unsafe at Any Speed*, a scathing attack on American car manufacturers for failing to make their automobiles safe to drive. Nader helped start a new form of opposition to capitalism, which has been called 'consumer activism'. It was based on the recognition that people were getting a raw deal from large corporations not as workers, but as consumers of their shoddy or dangerous products. Consumer activism has been especially important in campaigns over food safety.

first experience of organized protest as part of the hard-fought campaign for racial equality in the 1950s and 1960s. Another focus for protest was the threat of nuclear war. The Campaign for Nuclear Disarmament (CND) organized many mass protests, especially in the early 1960s. And, from the mid-1960s, American involvement in the Vietnam War led tens of thousands of people to attend mass protests and carry out acts of **civil disobedience**, convinced that there was no justification for the intervention that was causing military and civilian casualties on a massive scale.

American civil rights campaigner Martin Luther King Jr. (second from left) leads a protest march against unemployment in the 1960s.

Beatniks and hippies

There was also a wider sense of dissatisfaction with the prosperous 'consumer society' that postwar economic growth had created. The beatniks of the 1950s and hippies of the 1960s wanted to remove themselves from the drudgery of regular work and the money-ridden, **materialistic** 'rat-race' society. During the 1960s, experiments in communal living revived the ideals of the early socialists, with hundreds of young people attempting to establish small communities where all property was shared and the products of urban industrial society were shunned. Although few even among the young went to hippie extremes – loving and sharing tended to be experiences confined to a weekend at a pop festival, rather than everyday life – there was a widespread feeling that capitalism was delivering the goods, but not the good life.

Using the media

With no mass organization behind them, the 1960s radicals depended on the mass media, especially television, to give their words and actions a large-scale impact. Writing in the underground paper *International Times* in 1967, radical Tom McGrath said that the protesters 'have an instinctive understanding of... how to use the media to strongest advantage. In an instant-communication age, any act anywhere can be given worldwide significance if your communication link-up is efficient enough.' This lesson has been learned by contemporary anti-capitalists, who operate by creating a media spectacle which is a substitute for a mass organization of the kind old-fashioned socialists used to form.

The voice of the New Left

Clear-cut radical political ideas were restricted to a minority, mostly students at the fast-expanding universities. There the ideas of the 'New Left' were influential. These were **Marxists** who spoke the language of '**class conflict**' and 'revolutionary socialism'. They had no time for Soviet-style communism. Now one of the world's two 'superpowers', engaged in a contest with the United States to see who could produce the most powerful rockets and nuclear weapons, the Soviet Union was clearly not attempting to create any kind of ideal socialist society. To the New Left, the Soviet Union was a mirror image of Western capitalist society – different, perhaps, but equally oppressive and exploitative. Soviet leaders were elderly, white, male and dull. Youthful idealists looking forward to the revolutionary overthrow of capitalism were forced to search elsewhere for inspiration.

Some of the New Left put their faith in a series of revolutions in Third World countries. The guerrilla wars that had brought revolution to China, Cuba and North Vietnam were seen as an example that could be imitated across the developing world. Other New Leftists, including the Trotskyists, continued to have faith in revolution in the heartland of capitalism – Western Europe and North America. Even if Western factory workers would not revolt, the New Left hoped that others would, from students disillusioned with life under capitalism to victims of discrimination and oppression, such as poor African Americans and immigrant workers in Europe.

Young people protest against the Vietnam War in the 1960s.

Subverting capitalism

It was in the 1960s that the environmentally friendly bicycle became a symbol of opposition to the polluting, car-driving capitalist world. In 1965 the Dutch **anarchist** Provo (short for Provocation) group published a **manifesto** stating that 'we live in a... sick society', in which we are told 'what we should do, what we should consume...' As an act of subversion against this 'sick society', the Provos left thousands of white bicycles on the streets of Amsterdam. These were free for anyone to ride. People borrowing the bicycles were expected to leave them when they had finished their journey for someone else to use. This was supposed to stop people using cars – or in the Provos' words, end the 'terror of the motorized **bourgeoisie**'.

Until the second half of the 1960s, most people regarded the New Left talk of a possible 'revolution' in Western societies as evidence of how laughably out of touch they were with reality. But, as the number and scale of protests in different Western countries mounted, the possibility of revolutionary upheaval began to be more likely. This was especially true among students. By 1970, it was claimed, more than a million American students were prepared to describe themselves as 'revolutionaries'.

May 1968

The nearest to an actual revolution came in France in May 1968, when clashes between students and police in Paris sparked a general strike by workers which paralyzed the country for a month. In the same year in Eastern Europe, students and workers in former Czechoslovakia rebelled against communist rule. Students mounted a spectacular challenge to authority in Italy and West Germany, and confronted police on university campuses across the United States. In August, a confrontation between anti-Vietnam War protesters and police turned the centre of Chicago into a battleground.

May 1968: in Paris, police clashed with rioting students, many of whom wished for a new form of society to replace industrial capitalism.

The dominant mood of the 1968 revolts was of idealistic anarchism. One German student leader, Rudi Deutschke, said that the aim was 'an end to the power of people over people'. Most of the student radicals did not want to replace existing governments with a new government; they wanted no government at all. Not for them the example of earlier social reformers, who patiently built up

A young protester confronts a Soviet tank after the Soviet invasion of Czechoslovakia in 1968.

political movements to win mass support. Instead the 1968 radicals relied on direct action – especially confrontation with the police – and catchy slogans. The style of protest had an element of zaniness and fun that was quite different from the earnestness of traditional Marxism and socialism. In the United States, for example, the Yippies (Youth International Party) proposed putting forward a pig as a candidate in the elections for US president.

Asking for everything

Characteristic of the student revolts of the 1960s was a refusal to accept what are generally considered to be the normal realities of everyday life – the need to work, earn money, be less than happy much of the time. One famous 1960s slogan was: *'Be realistic – demand the impossible.'* Another, shouted during demonstrations, was: *'What do we want? Everything! When do we want it? Now!'*

43

In truth, there was no realistic chance that the student radicals, Marxists and anarchists could seriously overthrow the order of society. Soviet tanks crushed the student and worker rebellion in Czechoslovakia, while in France and the United States democratic elections in 1968 brought resounding victories for those most outspokenly opposed to the student revolts. The would-be revolutionaries in the West were revealed as a minority without broad public support.

Campaigns of terror

After their defeat in 1968, some radicals who remained committed to the violent overthrow of the capitalist system turned to terrorism. These post-1968 terrorist groups included the Red Brigades in Italy, the Baader-Meinhof Red Army Faction in West Germany, and the Weathermen (also known as the Weather Underground) in the United States.

Through the 1970s, such terrorist groups carried out bombings, kidnappings and assassinations. In Italy, for example, the Red Brigades kidnapped and murdered the prime minister, Aldo Moro, in 1978. The West German Baader-Meinhof group formed an alliance with Palestinian terrorists in the Middle East, carrying out some spectacular terrorist actions, including hijackings of airliners. The immediate terrorist wave had subsided by the end of the 1970s, but international terrorism was to be one of the most significant legacies of this period.

Tradition of protest

Far more of the 1968 radicals found more peaceful directions for their energies. In the 1970s protest movements continued to flourish, but mostly with more specific, less wide-ranging aims. The Women's Movement became a major force, launching an immensely effective assault on male authority and

Taking a new path

UK Green Party activist Jonathan Porritt explained that ecology parties were opposed to all existing political movements, whether pro-capitalist, communist, or social democrat, because these were all obsessed with maximizing industrial production:

'The politics of the Industrial Age, left, right, and centre, is like a three-lane motorway, with different vehicles in different lanes, but all heading in the same direction. Greens feel that it is the very direction that is wrong... the motorway of industrialization inevitably leads to the abyss – hence our decision to get off it, and seek an entirely different direction.'

privilege. Homosexuals campaigned for equal rights in the Gay Liberation movement. The fight against racism continued to concern many.

Perhaps most important, the ecology movement took off. The international environmental campaigning organization Greenpeace was founded in 1971, for example, and Green parties were founded which went on to win considerable electoral support, most notably in West Germany. The ecology movement threw down a challenge to both the capitalist and communist worlds, with their polluting industries and obsession with economic growth. The challenge was, in the main, to regulate industrial production in order to protect the world from further environmental destruction. The 1960s radicals had failed to make a revolution, but they had established a new tradition of protest that would not fade away.

This 1983 election poster for the German Green Party tells us that: 'We have only borrowed the Earth from our children'.

Opposing Global Capitalism

The 1980s was a decade of triumph for global **capitalism** and disaster for communism. This was a sudden and unexpected reversal. During the 1970s the capitalist world had still seemed on the defensive. Countries adopting, or taken over by, communist or communist-backed regimes in that decade included South Vietnam, Cambodia, Laos, Angola, Mozambique, Ethiopia, Nicaragua and Afghanistan. But the United States fought back by turning **guerrilla** war, traditionally a method employed by **left-wing** revolutionaries, against these left-wing regimes. US-backed guerrillas fought against the communist regimes in Nicaragua, Angola, Mozambique and Afghanistan. The Soviet army became engaged in a war against anti-communist guerrillas in Afghanistan that much resembled America's disastrous war in Vietnam.

Falling behind

Crucially, it was increasingly evident that the communist's state-controlled **economic system**, the only existing alternative to capitalism, was not working. In the state-controlled economies of the Soviet Union and Eastern Europe, output and living standards were falling further and further behind the capitalist West. Industry in communist countries was less efficient, and more technologically backward and

The killing fields

The possible dangers of pursuing a 'pure', non-capitalist society were demonstrated in Cambodia, Southeast Asia, after it was taken over by a peasant army of Khmer Rouge guerrillas in 1975. The Khmer Rouge set out to rid their country completely of Western capitalist influence. They considered the people of the country's one major city, Phnom Penh, hopelessly corrupted by contact with capitalism. These city dwellers were forced at gunpoint out into the country. There **collective farms** were established, where there was no private property and a totally communal life was imposed. For example, people were only allowed to eat in canteens – even picking berries from wild bushes to eat yourself was severely punished. Forced to work relentlessly in the fields from dawn to dusk, hundreds of thousands died of exhaustion, disease, brutal mistreatment, or summary execution.

polluting than that in the West. Although most people in the communist-ruled countries had secure employment and an adequate pension in old age, this security was at the expense of a lack of basic human rights and shortages of most consumer goods.

The collapse of communism

In the early 1980s the Solidarity **trade union** staged strikes and mass protests in communist-ruled Poland, demanding both political rights and better living conditions. Although no one knew it at the time, this was the first step towards the collapse of Soviet communism. In 1985 a dynamic, relatively young communist, Mikhail Gorbachev, became leader of the Soviet Union and introduced major reforms in an attempt to reverse economic decline. He only succeeded in creating chaos. As these reforms swept through the Soviet Union and Eastern Europe, popular protest mounted and communist rulers lost their grip on power.

In 1989, Germany's Berlin Wall – which had been built by the Soviet Union in 1961 to separate communist East Berlin from capitalist West Berlin – was broken down. Only two years later, the Soviet Communist Party was banned and the Soviet Union itself fell apart. China stayed under the control of the Communist Party, but its rulers largely abandoned communist economic policies, instead adopting free-market capitalism in an attempt to create economic growth.

The tearing down of the Berlin Wall in 1989 symbolized the failure of the communist political and economic system, and opened the way for the introduction of capitalism throughout the former communist countries.

Privatization

Communism had quite suddenly ceased to exist as a rival to capitalism. Meanwhile, social democracy in the West was also under attack. In Britain, for example, Margaret Thatcher, Conservative prime minister between 1979 and 1990, set out to reverse much of what the Labour movement had achieved over the years, cutting back on social security, pensions, and state-funded health care. She also returned state-owned industries to private ownership, in a process known as 'privatization', and curbed the power of the trade unions. To differing degrees, similar changes took place in most Western countries. At the same time, the kind of industries whose workers had provided the backbone of support for **socialism** – coal-mining, ship-building, iron and steel – were in sharp decline. **Social democrat** parties were obliged to water down the socialist element of their policies ever further to maintain support from voters.

Margaret Thatcher, British prime minister from 1979 to 1990, believed in a return to unbridled free-market capitalism. Her tough line with those who disagreed, especially trade unionists, earned her the nickname 'the Iron Lady'.

Globalization

As Soviet communism collapsed and democratic socialism waned, capitalism was entering an aggressive new phase. The capitalist system had always tended to create a 'global economy'. And there had always been a tendency for capitalist businesses to get bigger – merging or swallowing up smaller enterprises to create giant corporations. But these tendencies were taken far further than before in the process known as '**globalization**'.

Globalization essentially meant the whole world becoming a single economic unit, in which a small number of huge **multinational companies** would play a dominant role. It was at root a natural product of technological progress, which was making the world seem a smaller place. From the 1970s onward, the increasing use of computers and satellite communications made the movement of money and information from continent to continent almost instantaneous, while the growth of air travel allowed goods and people to move around the world far more quickly and easily than ever before. But this technological advance was accompanied by a deliberate political decision to return capitalism more or less to the classic form it had taken before 1914. Barriers to the movement of capital around the world were systematically removed and many trade barriers were lifted. This return to classic capitalism is known as 'neo-liberalism'. It showed a revival of the belief that if only governments would get out of the way and allow capitalists to trade and invest freely, prosperity would result.

Controlling global capitalism

One of the most unlikely critics of globalization to emerge in the 1990s was George Soros, a prominent financier who had made billions speculating on world financial markets. Soros argued that the global capitalist system needed to be brought under political control. He wrote:

'I do not want to abolish capitalism. In spite of its shortcomings, it is better than the alternatives.... [But] to stabilize and regulate a truly global economy we need some global system of political decision-making. In short, we need a global society to support our global economy.'

The power of the multinationals

The lifting of barriers on the movement of money and goods meant that multinational companies were independent of – in some ways far more powerful than – national governments. They could invest their cash and locate their factories or offices anywhere in the world – wherever labour was cheap and loosely regulated and governments were favourably disposed towards foreign businesses making profits. If workers asked for better wages and conditions or governments pursued even vaguely 'socialist' policies, the multinationals could take their investment and factories elsewhere.

The new global capitalism and 'neo-liberalism' were imposed on the governments and people of the developing world by pressure from international organizations. The International Monetary Fund (IMF) was an organization set up to support countries in economic difficulties and maintain financial stability across the world. Yet it would only lend money to countries that agreed to cut government spending by reducing their social programmes. The General Agreement on Tariff and Trade (GATT) and its successor from 1995, the World Trade Organization, pressed countries into removing barriers to the import of goods from abroad and abandoning all measures to support or subsidize their own locally based businesses.

To many people in smaller countries it seemed that the WTO was working to prevent them developing their economies, and to benefit the multinationals. For example, some banana growers on Caribbean islands, organized into cooperatives, were producing bananas on a small scale that they exported to Europe. The European Union imported these bananas on specially favourable terms, as a way of encouraging the Caribbean banana growers who were struggling to escape from poverty. But the WTO took the view that the European Union had to give equal treatment to bananas from large banana plantations run by American companies in countries such as Guatemala. If the European Union followed the WTO line then the Caribbean growers faced ruin, as they would not be able to compete with the American companies, which could produce bananas more cheaply.

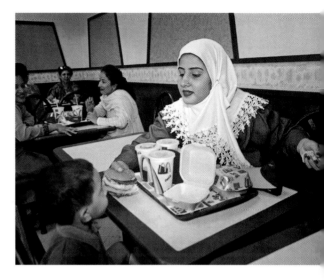

A McDonald's fast food outlet in Karachi, Pakistan – a striking example of the penetration of Western-based multinational businesses into every part of the world.

Anti-globalization

Supporters of globalization and neo-liberalism argued that it would lead to rapid economic growth across the world and offered all countries the best prospect of prosperity. But critics saw it as giving a free hand to multinationals to exploit the poorest of the Earth's people and destroy the natural environment. Throughout the 1990s anti-globalization became a fresh focus for protest movements.

Modern radical protest, established in the 1960s, had carried on through the decades, with ecological concerns increasingly holding centre stage. Protesters gathered wherever a new nuclear power plant, motorway or airport was being built, mobilizing public opinion against damage to the environment and threats to public health. Animal rights activists called for an end to factory-farming methods, and attacked the fur trade and the laboratory testing of cosmetics on animals.

Multinational burgers

A good example of the extraordinary expansion of multinational businesses over the last two decades is the growth of the McDonald's fast-food restaurant chain. By the early twenty-first century, there were McDonald's outlets in 120 countries. At one time, new branches were opening at the rate of four a day. It was estimated that, every day, one in 200 of the world's entire population ate at McDonald's.

Activists within the Women's Movement not only fought for equal rights for their sex but also called for an end to the aggressive and destructive relationship to the Earth. This, they argued, was typical of societies controlled by men, societies that were technology-oriented and bent on the 'conquest of nature'. More traditional socialist and **anarchist** concerns about poverty and inequality, and the dominance of the world by the power of money, had also continued to gain support.

Environmentalists

Globalization touched on all of these concerns. Environmentalists argued that the activities of multinationals had to be controlled if they were to be prevented from exhausting the Earth's non-renewable resources, destroying rain forests, polluting land and sea, and increasing global warming. Behind every new perceived threat to the environment – for example, from **GM** (genetically modified) **crops**, which became an issue in the late 1990s – there seemed to

Forests not for sale

Forest-dwellers in India have protested at attempts, supported by international organizations, to make commercial use of the forests. They stated:

'For the World Bank and the World Trade Organization, our forests are a marketable commodity. But for us, the forests are a home, our source of livelihood, the dwelling of our gods, the burial ground of our ancestors, the inspiration of our culture....We will not let you sell our forests. So go back from our forests and our country.'

Greenpeace activists attack an experimental planting of GM maize in eastern England in 1999. Protesters saw GM crops as an example of big business threatening the environment for profit.

be a multinational company trying to increase its profits. At the same time, the question of inequality continued to plague capitalism as it had from the earliest days. Capitalism could create ever more wealth, but at the same time always seemed to be creating an ever greater gap between the richest and poorest. Welfare spending cuts and other measures imposed by the IMF were a direct attack on the living standards of some of the world's poorest people. And, in the 1990s, poor countries were actually paying more to the richest countries in debt repayments than they were receiving in aid.

Issues such as world poverty and environmental damage were acknowledged as subjects for discussion by governments, by well-established pressure groups such as Greenpeace and by the **United Nations**, through bodies such as the UN Commission on Sustainable Development. But anti-capitalist radicals felt more direct action was needed. A wave of anti-globalization protests grew during the 1990s. These were directly descended in style from the protests of the 1960s (see pages 38 to 45). In the same way, they were not the work of mass organizations with clear leadership and political programmes. Instead they were the work of different small groups, loosely brought together by a commitment to acts of **civil disobedience** or confrontation with the authorities.

The Ogoni oilfields

Protesters in the developing world sometimes faced extreme violence from the authorities. In Nigeria, for example, the minority Ogoni people of the Niger delta claimed that multinational oil companies exploiting oil reserves on their territory had created an ecological disaster. In return for seeing the fish and shellfish they used to eat poisoned by oil slicks, and their land crisscrossed with massive pipelines, the Ogoni argued they had received nothing – neither jobs nor the investment to provide basic services such as electricity or clean drinking water. But when the Ogoni organized a protest movement, the Nigerian authorities reacted with great severity. In 1995 nine leaders of the movement, including writer Ken Saro-Wiwa, were found guilty on trumped-up charges and executed by hanging.

The protesters

In Europe and North America, the protesters were a mix of **Marxist** revolutionary socialists, radical trade unionists, women's groups, environmental activists, anarchists, and animal rights groups. In the developing world, resistance to global capitalism came mostly from the rural population, who saw their way of life and living standards threatened by the new wave of capitalist economic development. Prominent among groups confronting capitalism in the Third World were the Zapatistas, representing Indian peasants in Mexico, the Landless movement representing the poorest people of Brazil, and various farmers' organizations in India, especially the Narmada Bachao Andolan (NBA), formed to resist the building of the Narmada dam.

Carnival against capital

Making extensive use of the Internet as a method of organization from the mid-1990s, networks were formed both among the groups in the industrialized countries and in the developing world. This led to coordinated actions such as international days of protest. On 18 June 1999, for example, a 'carnival against capital' was held in cities around the world, including London and New York. Each May Day became an occasion for an attempt to disrupt life in major cities. But above all the focus of protest became the increasingly frequent meetings of world leaders and multinational trade regulators, which were considered essential precisely because of the need to deal with issues raised by the global economy. Protesters made

Globalized protest

The anti-capitalist movement was itself partly a product of globalization – the shrinking of the world through electronic communications and air transport. The Internet made possible the direct link-up between small groups in many parts of the world without any cumbersome organization involving leaders and membership cards. International protesters were also able to assemble swiftly at any point in the world to stage a demonstration. For example, anti-capitalists from Mexico, Bangladesh, or Thailand would take part in protests in the Czech Republic, Spain or Canada. This was sometimes described as 'globalization from the bottom up', as opposed to capitalism's 'globalization from the top down'.

The 'carnival against capital' held in cities around the world, including London, June 1999.

their presence felt from the Seattle meeting of the WTO in 1999 (see page 4) to the American Free Trade Area summit in Quebec in April 2001, the European Union summit in Barcelona in March 2002 and the Earth summit in South Africa in August 2002.

In many ways the protesters were a rag-tag army compared with the disciplined ranks and mass movements of earlier socialism. Yet in another they were extremely influential, since the protesters were only one wing of a movement of criticism of globalization that also included such respectable bodies as United Nations commissions, major **non-governmental organizations**, and many governments of countries in the developing world. Whether influence could be turned into action was a more difficult question.

Anti-capitalist principles

Peoples' Global Action (PGA), one of the most prominent groupings in the anti-capitalist movement, describes itself as a network coordinating the struggle of 'all those who fight the destruction of humanity and the planet by capitalism'. The declared principles of the PGA are typical of the anti-capitalist movement. They include: 'a very clear rejection of capitalism, imperialism and **feudalism**, all trade agreements, institutions and governments that promote destructive globalization'; the rejection of 'all forms of domination and discrimination including... **patriarchy**, racism, and religious fundamentalism...'; and a belief in 'a confrontational attitude... direct action and civil disobedience'.

Into the Twenty-First Century

By the beginning of the twenty-first century, New York, the largest city in the United States, the home of the **United Nations**, the World Trade Centre and many **multinational corporations**, was widely seen as the hub of global **capitalism**. On 11 September 2001, Islamic fundamentalist terrorists destroyed the World Trade Centre, killing thousands of innocent people.

11 September 2001: terrorists destroy New York's World Trade Centre, symbolic hub of global capitalism.

This was in a sense an 'anti-capitalist' gesture, inspired by the desire to destroy the current American-dominated world system. Most Muslims and members of the Western anti-capitalist movement did not support the 11 September attack. They rejected both **Islamic fundamentalism** and terrorism. But many nonetheless regarded it as the expression of a justified anger, an understandable reaction to the injustice that condemned much of the world's population to powerlessness and poverty.

Defenders of capitalism

Pro-capitalists argue that this attitude is irrational. They take a positive view of capitalism's past and future impact on the world. They point out that it has brought great prosperity to a

Learn to love wealth

In 1998, in his book *Eat the Rich*, the American **right-wing** journalist P. J. O'Rourke vigorously expresses the pro-capitalist position. He argues that the quickest way to reduce poverty in the developing world is to let capitalists make as much money as possible, without worrying about equality:

'If we want the whole world to be rich, we need to start loving wealth. In the difference between poverty and plenty, the problem is the poverty, not the difference.'

No more hunger

Speaking in 2000, Eric Hobsbawm, a distinguished historian highly critical of capitalism, argued nonetheless that living standards of the world's population have improved because of the global economy:

'We have today three times the [world] population there was at the start of the twentieth century, and all these people are physically stronger, taller, longer-living and healthier. They suffer less hunger and famine, enjoy a higher income, and have an immeasurably greater access to goods and services.... This is also true of poorer countries.... Hunger in most of the world... is no longer something that human beings are obliged to live with.'

considerable part of the world's population, notably in Europe and North America, and say that over time it will do the same for the rest of the world. After all, some countries in the Third World that have encouraged private enterprise – for example, South Korea and Taiwan – have achieved a spectacular rise in living standards in a few decades.

Many pro-capitalists do not reject the concerns raised by the anti-capitalist movement. They accept, to a greater or lesser degree, the need to limit damage to the environment or to help eradicate world poverty. But they believe that these goals can be achieved either by mildly reforming the way capitalism works through government intervention and regulation, or even by *more* capitalism – for example, by making environmentally friendly projects profitable for business corporations to carry out.

Taiwanese workers assemble motherboards for computers. Countries such as Taiwan and South Korea have been successful modern examples of capitalist enterprise, experiencing a dramatic rise in living standards.

The anti-capitalist arguments

Anti-capitalists argue that free-market capitalism must inevitably impoverish many to profit a few. They point to the environmental damage being caused by multinational corporations and the fact that they do not seem prepared to do anything to control it. They point to the **undemocratic** nature of the global system, in which even where elected governments exist, they are largely powerless in the face of global capitalism. They see poverty increasing, not decreasing, as **globalization** spreads – witness the mass of **economic migrants** trying to enter the world's richer states from the poorer ones. Russia is a good example of the possible negative effects of capitalism, for the change from communism to free-market capitalism in the 1990s has led to a sharp rise in poverty and a sharp fall in life expectancy.

Traditional rights

In some ways the anti-capitalist movement can be seen as conservative, rather than revolutionary. Most of the protests are an attempt to resist change and defend traditional rights. These rights may be the way of life of forest dwellers and peasant farmers in the developing world or, in the developed world, the hard-won rights of trade unionists, the welfare state, or unspoilt countryside threatened by road-building.

However, anti-capitalism is also inspired by a vision of the future that has much, though not everything, in common with the old socialist tradition. It is a

All life is precious

In 1999 the League of Revolutionaries for a New America expressed the view that capitalism was the obstacle blocking the way to a better world:

'For the first time in history, technological innovations have given society the means to produce an absolute abundance.... The new wealth generated by these changes is not being shared by all. Instead, obscene riches are being accumulated at one pole of society, while a more and more brutal poverty is created at the other.... Our society can either move to a police state that upholds repression and enforces suffering, or it can move forward to a new stage of human development that cherishes and nurtures the lives of all.'

Changing history

Speaking in the 1990s of the many different movements opposing capitalism, from peasant groups in Mexico and Brazil to anti-globalization protesters in the industrialized countries, American radical Noam Chomsky said:

'If these diverse, dispersed movements everywhere manage to create bonds of solidarity and support... together they will be able to change the course of contemporary history.'

vision of humans living in harmony with their environment and with one another, respecting animals as well as their fellow human beings, tending planet Earth to create a sustainable future. Economic growth will still take place, but in a form that is not destructive of the Earth's resources and that is beneficial to all people, not just a few. And people in local communities will have power over their own lives, building links with other communities across the world.

The fall of global capitalism, so often predicted over the last two centuries, looks as unlikely at the start of the third millennium as it ever did. The anti-capitalist movement might help set the agenda on world poverty or environmental issues, but it does not imagine it will 'seize power' by overthrowing national governments. Any form of world revolution is a distant concept. Yet the vision of a better, even ideal, world of equal sharing, peace, mutual respect and harmony continues to exist as a driving force in contemporary anti-capitalist movements.

Confrontations between riot police and anti-capitalist protesters looked set to continue through the first decade of the twenty-first century.

Date List

1811 'Luddites', poor hand-weavers in England opposed to the introduction of weaving machinery, attack factories and destroy machines.

1813 Robert Owen publishes *A New View of Society*, one of the earliest statements of socialist views.

1834 The Tolpuddle Martyrs are found guilty of forming a trade union, and deported to Australia.

1839 Britain launches the first Opium War against China, to force the Chinese to open their ports to foreign trade.

1844 Britain's first cooperative store is set up in Rochdale, Lancashire.

1848 *The Communist Manifesto*, written by Karl Marx and his associate Friedrich Engels, calls for a workers' revolution to overthrow capitalism.

1864 The International Working Men's Association, or First International, is founded to coordinate the actions of socialists and revolutionaries in different countries.

1867 Karl Marx publishes the first volume of *Das Kapital* (Capital), his immensely influential analysis of, and attack on, capitalism.

1871 A popular uprising in Paris creates the Paris Commune, a revolutionary government that is soon crushed with great loss of life.

1889 The Second International is founded, an international organization which is joined by most socialist parties.

1903 A split in the Russian Social Democratic Party leaves V. I. Lenin as head of the Bolshevik faction.

1905 International Workers of the World, an anarchist union movement dedicated to class war, is founded in the USA.

1906 The British Labour Party, originally founded in 1900 as the Labour Representation Committee, has twenty-six MPs elected to Parliament.

1914-18 The First World War.

1917 The Bolshevik seizure of power in the Russian Revolution establishes the world's first long-lived anti-capitalist government, leading to the formation of the Soviet Union in 1923.

1924 The first Labour government comes to power in Britain; it lasts less than a year.

1929 A stock market crash marks the beginning of the Great Depression.

1929 Dictator Josef Stalin initiates rapid industrialization and state control of agriculture in the Soviet Union.

1933 US President F. D. Roosevelt initiates the New Deal, abandoning many of the principles of free-market capitalism in response to the Depression and mass unemployment.

1939-45 The Second World War.

1945 Victory against Nazi Germany leaves the Soviet Union in control of central Europe.

1945 A Labour government is elected in Britain with a large majority; it takes the major industries into public ownership and founds a welfare state.

1949 Communists led by Mao Tse-tung take power in China; an alternative system to capitalism prevails from the Pacific Ocean to central Europe.

Resources

1959 Guerrilla leader Fidel Castro takes power in Cuba, soon declaring his allegiance to communism.

1968 Riots and protests, in which left-wing students play a leading part, sweep Western Europe and North America.

1971 The environmental campaigning organization Greenpeace is founded.

1978 The Italian prime minister, Aldo Moro, is kidnapped and murdered by members of the Red Brigades.

1980 Deng Xiao-ping leads China towards capitalist-style free-market economic policies, although the Communist Party remains in power.

1985 Mikhail Gorbachev becomes head of the Soviet Union and tries to reform its economic and political system.

1989 The fall of the Berlin Wall marks the collapse of Communist government across central Europe.

1991 The Soviet Union ceases to exist.

1995 The World Trade Organization (WTO) is founded.

1999 Anti-capitalist riots rock Seattle during a WTO summit meeting.

July 2001 An anti-capitalist protester is killed during clashes with police at an economic summit of world leaders in Genoa, Italy.

Sept 2001 Terrorists crash hijacked airliners into the World Trade Centre in New York and the Pentagon.

March 2002 Mass demonstrations take place during a European summit meeting in Barcelona, Spain.

Nov 2002 A huge anti-capitalism march takes place peacefully in Florence, Italy.

Capitalism, Reg Grant, Ideas of the Modern World series, Wayland, 2001

Global Debt, Teresa Garlake, 21st Century Debates series, Wayland, 2007

People Power, Campaigns and Causes, Richard Tames and David Downing, Heinemann, 2003

The Communist Manifesto, Karl Marx, 1848

Fiction and humour

Animal Farm, George Orwell, 1945

The Soul of Man Under Socialism, Oscar Wilde, 1891

Eat the Rich, P. J. O'Rourke, Picador, 1999

Gasping, Ben Elton, Samuel French, 1998

Glossary

anarchists
those who reject all forms of government and authority, wanting to live in small self-governing communities.

anarcho-syndicalist
member of a movement that wanted to use trade unions as a basis for the violent overthrow of capitalism.

bourgeoisie
in the Marxist view of capitalist society, the bourgeoisie is the social class that owns the means of production – factories, machines, etc. – and financial capital.

bourgeois rule
according to Marxist thinkers, in a capitalist society the bourgeoisie (see above) controls the government, which it uses to make laws that serve its own interests.

bureaucrats
the officials who run government departments and state organizations.

capitalism
an economic system based upon private ownership of business and trade.

civil disobedience
a form of non-violent protest involving the refusal to obey – or the deliberate breaking of – laws that are regarded as unjust.

class conflict
conflict between different groups in society, especially between industrial workers and factory owners, seen by Marxists as having fundamentally opposed economic interests.

collective farm
a large farm run by the state, created by taking over the land of independent peasant farmers.

colonial power
a state that runs other countries as part of an empire.

commune
a group of people living together and sharing property and responsibility for work on an equal basis.

democracy
a political system in which government is run by representatives elected by the people.

dictatorial
exercising absolute power.

economic migrants
people who move around their country or around the world in search of work and a better standard of living.

economic system
the way the production and distribution of goods and services is organized.

exploit
in an economic context, to pay someone far less for their work or for the goods they produce than these are really worth.

extremist
someone opposed to compromise or half-measures.

feudalism
an economic and social system dominated by an aristocracy of landowners to whom their 'inferiors' owe dues and service.

free trade
international trade that is free of government-imposed restrictions.

globalization
the breaking down of all barriers to the movement of money or goods between countries, in theory turning the whole world into a single economic unit.

GM crops
genetically modified crops – crops that have had their genetic material altered by scientists to give them new characteristics.

guerrilla
a soldier who fights in small-scale hit-and-run warfare; not a member of a regular army.

ideology
a set of ideas that expresses the beliefs of a political movement or a government.

imperialist
a person who extends the power or influence of one nation over others, as in an empire.

Islamic fundamentalism
a movement in Muslim countries that advocates a return to the original principles of the Islamic faith, rejecting any compromise with the modern world or Western capitalism.

labor union
the American term for trade union.

left-wing
the term used for radical, liberal, socialist, communist, or anarchist political groups or ideas.

manifesto
a statement of a political programme.

Marxist
person or government taking some version of the thoughts of Karl Marx as the basis for their political ideas or political system.

mass movements
political movements involving many people.

materialistic
excessively devoted to making money or accumulating possessions.

militant
a very active and uncompromising political activist or movement.

military coup
a seizure of power by the armed forces.

military regimes
governments run by officers of the armed forces.

multinational business
a large company that operates in many countries across the world.

non-governmental organizations (NGOs)
organizations that are independent of control by any government.

patriarchy
a system in which men dominate society and women occupy an inferior position.

political activist
someone actively involved in campaigning, protests, and other political action.

proletariat
Marxist term for the industrial working class – factory workers, miners, etc.

propaganda
information designed to advance a cause or serve the interests of a government.

right-wing
the term used for political groups or ideas opposed to communism, socialism, radicalism or anarchism.

shareholder
person who owns shares in a company, usually having bought them on the stock market.

social democrat
person who believes, at least to some degree, in socialism, but not at the expense of democracy or individual freedom.

socialism
an alternative economic and social system to capitalism – in which extremes of wealth and poverty are eradicated and the economy is run for the good of the community, rather than for individual profit.

stock market
a place where shares in companies are bought and sold.

trade blockade
preventing goods being imported into or exported out of a country.

trade union
an organization formed by a group of working people to represent their interests in negotiations or conflict with their employers.

Tsarist regime
the government of Russia before the Revolution of 1917, when the country was ruled by an Emperor, the Tsar.

undemocratic
a situation in which people have no control over decisions that affect their lives and no right to elect or dismiss those who take such decisions.

underdevelopment
a term used to describe the situation of countries whose people are poorer than those of the world's richest states, with less productive economies and inferior health care, education, and transport services.

United Nations
an international body, formed in 1945, with almost all the world's countries as members. It sets international standards, aims to resolve conflicts and manages relief and development programmes.

utopian socialist
a term sometimes used for early socialists who concentrated on the vision of a future ideal society (called 'utopia') rather than on the realities of social conflict.

Index